GONG
BASS
THEORY

GEORG HÄRNSTEN EGG

CONTENT

Copyright © 2018 Georg Härnsten Egg

Text and music notation: Georg Härnsten Egg

Notation design: Ludvig Rosvall

Book design: Joel Fox Apelgren

Layout: Helena Öhman, STUDIO INDIGO

Photography: Gustaf Sandholm Andersson

ISBN 978-91-639-8192-0

INTRODUCING GONG BASS THEORY

GONG BASS THEORY IS A NEW APPROACH to double bass drumming, using a single pedal and a Gong Bass drum played with the left hand.

This book is the result of many years of exploring and developing this technique.

The idea is simple: to be able to play double bass music with only one pedal. To do this I use a Gong Bass drum on the left side of my hi-hat, which I play with my left hand. People often ask me why, and I don't really have a good answer except that I like it, and it's different. There are some benefits though: I can still play the hi-hat with my left foot while playing intricate double bass patterns with my right foot and left hand. To me, this adds a bit of funk and groove to a style of music that sometimes sounds a little robotic.

Some negative aspects are that it can be harder to hit the strokes with an equal volume level and that some patterns that contain a lot of snare drum hits can get very difficult to play, since the left hand plays both the snare drum and the Gong Bass.

The background story goes like this: after the third Dynazty album, *Sultans of Sin*, we decided we wanted to take our music into a heavier and more metal direction. I had always played a single pedal like my heroes Vinny Appice and Ian Paice, among others. We added more bass drum notes to our new songs, first maybe three in a row, which is one too many to be done with the foot alone, so I figured I could do that if I just played one note on the floor tom. This worked all right, but then we kept adding more notes. With the increasing amount of bass drum notes, the floor tom just didn't sound right, so I got myself a Gong Bass drum and started experimenting. Not only did this require a lot of practice, but also a lot of trial and error. There are many ways of playing every pattern, every groove, and I had to explore them all to find out what felt and sounded the best to me.

After a few months I started seeing some constant factors I could use to build this technique upon. For example: a straight 16th note double bass groove is a paradiddle between the right foot and the left hand.

There are two reasons for this:
1. I like to start every beat possible with my right foot, since it gives me stability.
2. This way I get two right foot notes before I hit the snare drum, which gives me time to move my left arm from the Gong Bass to the snare drum and get a good solid hit.

In this book I have notated some basic grooves that I use a lot, some exercises that can be used for fills and improvisation, and a lot of Dynazty parts from our albums *Renatus* and *Titanic Mass*.

All of these patterns can be viewed as coordination exercises if you don't have any interest in playing Gong Bass, and all the Gong Bass hits can be moved around the kit for new and cool ideas.

I hope you find some sort of inspiration from reading this, and I also want to thank all the drummers around the world who have contacted me and requested notations for parts of Dynazty songs – you definitely helped me get this done. Keep requesting! I can add new songs in the future and appreciate other drummers helping me choose.

Stockholm, June 2018
Georg Härnsten Egg

NOTE KEY

Gong Bass drum   Floor tom   Tom-tom   Hi-hat/crash/ride/china

Bass drum   Snare drum

Drums: *Mapex Saturn V*
10" & 12" toms, 16" floor tom, 18" Gong Bass drum,
14" x 5.5" snare drum, 22" x 18" bass drum.

Cymbals: *Zildjian*
14" K Hybrid hi-hat, 18" K Dark crash, 18" K EFX,
19" A Ultra Hammered china, 21" A Mega Bell ride.

GROOVES

IN THIS CHAPTER I PRESENT some patterns that I commonly use when playing various double bass tunes as a freelance drummer. The basic patterns are quite simple and stay the same in each segment. They are played with the right foot on the bass drum pedal and the left hand on the Gong Bass and snare drum.

The thing that changes in each bar is the right hand pattern, which can be played on a hi-hat, ride, china, crash, cowbell, or whatever! Some of these patterns turn into challenging coordination exer-cises and the goal is just to feel comfortable enough with the basic pattern so that the right hand is free to do whatever you want on top of it all.

In addition to this I suggest that you try using your left foot on the hi-hat pedal for each groove. Play for example quarter notes, eighth notes, and off-beat eighth notes. This will improve your coordination skills and add funk to the grooves.

Good luck!

In the studio with QFT

Some basic 16th note double bass grooves. The paradiddle between the right foot and left hand stays intact, but the right hand ride pattern changes. Try keeping the left foot hi-hat on quarter notes, eighth notes and off-beat eighth notes.

Right hand removed. Great exercise for balance!

Some more patterns following the same recipe:

In this last exercise the right hand plays dotted eighth notes, which makes the pattern turn around after six quarter notes.

Half-time grooves. The basic pattern here is a triple paradiddle between the right foot and left hand, the right hand ride pattern changes. Left foot hi-hat: Quarter notes, eighth notes and off-beat eighth notes.

In this pattern the right hand just follows the right foot:

A bunch of triplet grooves. The basic pattern consists of single strokes between the right foot and left hand. The right hand ride pattern changes, try keeping the left foot hi-hat on quarter notes.

Half-time shuffle grooves. The basic pattern here is a double paradiddle between the right foot and the left hand. Try keeping the left foot hi-hat on quarter notes, half notes and off-beat quarter notes.

FILLS AND IMPROVISATION

MY IDEA OF IMPROVISING with a Gong Bass setup is that it should be basically the same as a drummer who uses a double pedal or a double bass drum setup: to be used here and there, a little or a lot.

In this chapter I give some examples of patterns to use, mostly based upon single strokes between the right foot and the left hand. Single strokes are the easiest way to reach loud volume, which is something I tend to want when playing heavy music.

When developing single strokes, I've found that relaxation and exactitude in technique give me a better result than pushing speed. Start slow and build balance before increasing the tempo!

Remember to keep the left foot hi-hat on quarter notes, eighth notes and off-beat eighth notes during the exercises. This will help you build the balance that you need to be able to play these patterns at a high tempo, yet staying relaxed and precise.

On tour with Dynazty

A simple yet effective fill:

A pattern with an increasing amount of single strokes:

Fill from Dawn of Your Creation, last chorus. The tempo on the album is 200 bpm:

Here is an exercise I used a lot to develop single strokes.
The pattern is taken from Future Breed Machine by Meshuggah. The right hand plays the snare
and ride on this one, so that the left hand can focus only on the Gong Bass.
Try different right hand patterns and try keeping the left foot hi-hat on quarter notes,
eighth notes and off-beat eighth notes.

Another fill. Try starting it in different places and use it to improvise!

I use the following pattern a lot. Use small bits of it to improvise or play the whole pattern over and over while practicing. Remember to try keeping the left foot hi-hat on quarter notes, eighth notes and off-beat eighth notes. I use this in the drum solo on the song New Frontier by The Paralydium Project.

Some triplet fills!

Here are some exercises for playing grooves that include three-stroke bursts, such as
Incarnation by Dynazty or Bleed by Meshuggah.
A three-stroke burst between Gong Bass and right foot can be done in six different ways.
I like to use four of these:

The following patterns are good as a foundation, but the possibilities are more or less limitless.
Try different variations, different ride patterns, different left foot hi-hat patterns.
Experiment and improvise! Skip the Gong Bass and play the left hand around the kit, or skip
the ride and play the right hand around the kit!

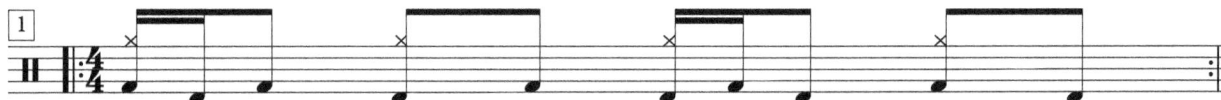

DYNAZTY PARTS

I'VE CHOSEN A FEW PARTS of different Dynazty songs that I wanted to transcribe and some that have been requested by fellow drummers. These are some of the more intricate and challenging parts that can be found on albums *Renatus* (2014) and *Titanic Mass* (2016).

As you will see, a lot of the 16th note based grooves come from the paradiddle pattern shown in the first chapter, just skipping or adding some notes here and there. So the basic paradiddle groove is a great foundation to build from if you want to master these parts.

I didn't notate the left foot hi-hat, because I don't think it's necessary. However, on almost all of these parts I play quarter notes on the hi-hat with my left foot, due to the high tempo.

In Cross the Line, where the tempo is a little lower, I play off-beat eighth notes on the hi-hat with the left foot to add a bit of extra spice.

Dynazty live in Stockholm

The Human Paradox: Riff, played on crash.

170 bpm

The Human Paradox: Half-time, played on crash.

170 bpm

Starlight: Riff, played on crash.

160 bpm

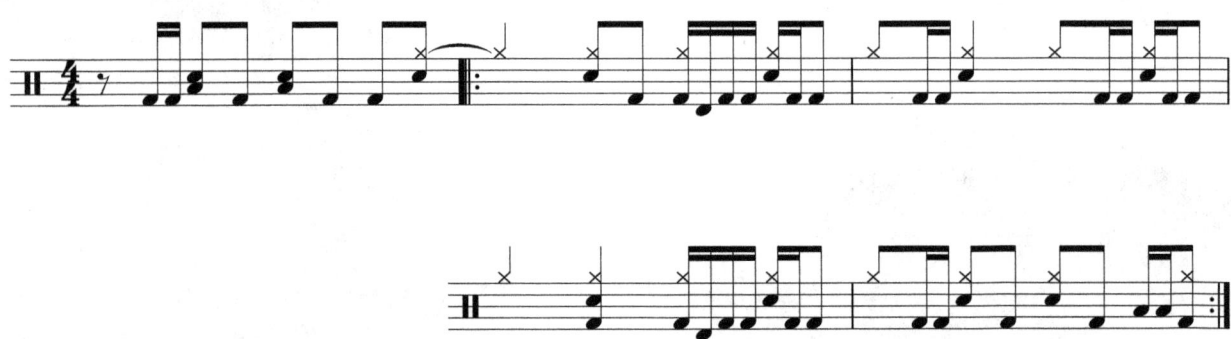

Starlight: Pre-chorus, played on ride bell and hi-hat.

160 bpm

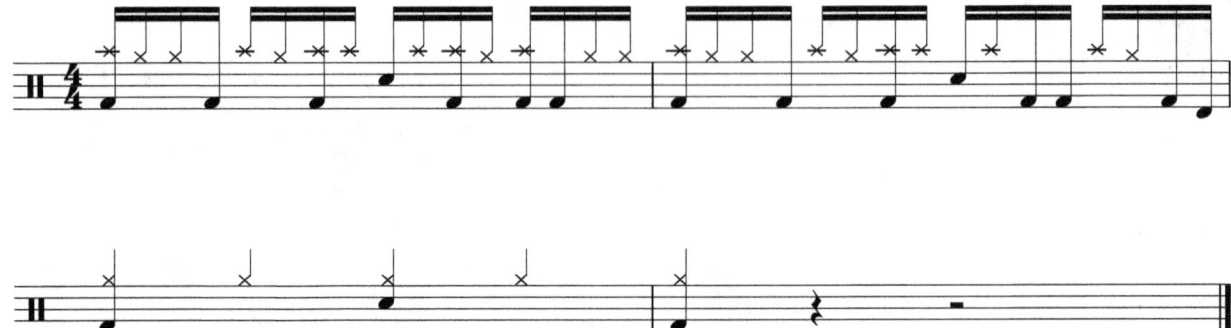

Break into the Wild: Verse, played on hi-hat.

145 bpm

Break into the Wild: Bridge, played on hi-hat the first time and crash the second time.

145 bpm

Keys to Paradise: Bridge, played on china.

160 bpm

Cross the Line: Intro riff, played on crash.

125 bpm

China

Titanic Mass: Second verse, played on hi-hat.

155 bpm

Roar of the Underdog: Riff, played on crash.

160 bpm

Unholy Deterrent: Riff, played on crash.

140 bpm

Unholy Deterrent: Middle part, played on ride bell. The groove is the same as in the riff, except for the right hand pattern that now instead follows the right foot.

140 bpm

Unholy Deterrent: Guitar solo, played on hi-hat.

140 bpm

Run Amok: Pre-chorus, played on ride bell.

160 bpm

Incarnation: Riff, played on crash. Notice the few floor tom hits, they are played with the right hand to give a little help to the right foot which has a lot to do in this song. The floor tom hits can be traded for right foot bass drum notes if you have a really fast foot! Anyway, this is how I play it:

200 bpm

AFTERWORD

I HOPE THIS BOOK HAS GIVEN YOU some new ideas on the drum set and inspiration to further explore the possibilities on our instrument. It would be interesting to see other drummers adapt this style of playing and all the crazy stuff that might be created in the process!

It's an ever ongoing process. With each new song that my bands write I'm forced to transform the double bass notes into playable Gong Bass patterns. If it weren't for them constantly pushing my limits, I don't think this book would have come about. Therefore I'd like to say a big thank you to Dynazty, The Paralydium Project and QFT, not only for creating awesome drum parts but also for believing in me and letting me stick to this odd and previously untried technique, that has sometimes created problems with sound technicians and has led many to ask: "Why don't you just get a double pedal?" My answer is that I like that it's different. By trying

something different we can find new ideas and ways of making music on our instrument, which in turn can help us bring the art form forward.

A big thank you to EM Nordic, Mapex drums and Zildjian cymbals for your support through the years.

As I mentioned in the beginning of this book, I'd be happy to receive requests on songs that you want transcribed. I will likely publish a second volume in the future, when I feel that I have enough new material to make it worth checking out.

I wish you all good luck in your drumming lives!

ABOUT THE AUTHOR

GEORG HÄRNSTEN EGG IS A DRUMMER, clinician, teacher and author from Stockholm, Sweden. He has worked with prominent groups and artists including Dynazty, The Paralydium Project, QFT, Joe Lynn Turner, Brian May and Kee Marcello.

Gong Bass Theory is Georg's first instructional book, introducing a new approach to double bass drumming, using a single pedal and a Gong Bass drum played with the left hand.

ACKNOWLEDGEMENTS

Photography by Gustaf Sandholm Andersson.
Notation design by Ludvig Rosvall.
Book design by Joel Fox Apelgren.

Contact:
gongbasstheory@gmail.com
www.gongbasstheory.com

ENDORSEMENTS